HOW TO BRAND NEW

A BRANDING ROAD MAP TO STAND OUT, DOMINATE, AND PROSPER!

BOAZ RAUCHWERGER

SPEAKER OF THE YEAR FOR VISTAGE INTERNATIONAL, THE WORLD'S LARGEST ORGANIZATION OF CEO'S.

Published by

Boaz Power Press
Woodland Hills, CA.
A Division of Boaz Power Corp.

Printed in Canada.

Most Boaz Power Press titles are available at special quantity discounts for bulk purchases for sales promotions, premiums, fundraising, and educational use. Special versions or book excerpts can also be created to fit specific needs.

For more information, please write:

Special Markets
Boaz Power Press
20600 Ventura Blvd., Ste. 2409
Woodland Hills, CA 91364

Call or email:
619-723-3007
Boaz@BoazPower.com
Visit us online at: www.boazpower.com

ISBN 978-0-578-51787-2

About the Author

Boaz Rauchwerger is an internationally-known, award-winning speaker, author, and consultant. He is the Speaker of the Year for Vistage International, the world's largest organization of CEO's and has spoken for such companies as American Airlines, Xerox, and Toyota.

He is the founder of Boaz Power Corp., a worldwide organization that serves a variety of client companies with expertise in branding, marketing, communications, team-building, and high performance.

Born in Israel, Boaz immigrated to the United States when he was nine. Even though he did not speak a word of English at the time, by the time he was in high school he had become a newscaster on a large radio station in the Midwest.

He has worked in radio and television news, was a newspaper publisher, a CEO, owned his own advertising agency, a network television producer, and has spoken before audiences worldwide. Boaz appeared regularly, as a high performance coach, on the Lifetime Television program *"The Balancing Act"*.

Table of Contents

Introduction

Welcome to your new future!

What if you could do a few simple things that could have the potential to take you to a new level of success? What if there was a way to create a brand new you, where doors to great opportunities would literally open up in front of you? Where you could gain more business and close more sales?

If you work for a company, or are in business for yourself, one of the keys to your greater success is branding. What kind of impression do you make on other people and on your market? What kind of a lasting affect do you have on others that will make them want to do business with you, now and in the future? What differentiates you from your competition? How are you making meaningful connections with your customers?

Most people have no idea of how to create a powerful brand that will make them stand out, get them to dominate their industry, and help them prosper. That's what this book is all about. Branding is the way people perceive you, in person, on the phone, in social media, through advertising, on your website, or through broadcast media. I'll share with you great ideas that can make you much more memorable in all of those areas.

My mother was from Poland, father from Austria. They both went to Palestine as pioneers in 1935, to help build a new country. I was born in Israel. My family immigrated to the United States when I was nine. We lived in Oklahoma for many years, and I moved to California in 1985 because of the weather. I lived in San Diego, Orange County, and now Los Angeles.

I've had a variety of careers that have brought me to this

point. I've been a radio and television newscaster, a newspaper publisher, a CEO, a builder of homes, a professional speaker, and I owned my own advertising agency. I like marketing and branding, and we're about to discuss ways to market you better than ever before! These days anyone who doesn't stand out, and have a unique branding program that gets attention and is remembered, can be left behind.

In nearly 20 years as a professional speaker, I've become the Speaker of the Year for Vistage International, the world's largest organization of CEO's. I've conducted nearly 2,000 seminars for their groups in the U.S., Canada, Mexico, Great Britain, and destinations beyond.

In doing this, I've had the most amazing laboratory to work with as I tested branding and marketing ideas with over 25,000 CEO's. At this point, I believe I've spoken before more CEO's than anyone in the world. I have gotten to see what ideas worked and which ones did not. I've also had the privilege of speaking for such companies as American Airlines, Xerox, and Toyota.

In this book, I will share with you the most productive branding ideas that I've identified from my extensive experience with the CEO's in Vistage. These ideas are not wishful thinking. They're ideas that CEO's in my audiences have tested, gotten great results, and reported back to me on their value.

If you're looking for secrets to becoming a social media guru in order to expand your brand, this is not your book. You can hire someone for that, or get one cheaply called "a teenager". Many of my ideas are old-fashioned. Some are corny. But, if an old, corny idea could bring your company an extra million dollars, would you be willing to listen to an old idea? I would think you would. Some of the ideas I share have been worth that, and more, to those who used them.

This is not a lengthy book. There is no need for that. It's going to be an easy read and you'll be able to implement some of the ideas within minutes of reading them. I simply ask that you report back to me, as many CEO's have, to let me know how some of the ideas changed your life for the better, and how you became BRAND NEW. My email address is Boaz@ Boazpower.com.

However, before we get to the ideas, I need to take your attitude to a higher level so you can take full advantage of these ideas. I'm also going to help you identify your WHY, a reason for you to succeed bigger. I teach out of two books and I don't make a penny when you buy either one: **"How to Win Friends and Influence People"** by Dale Carnegie, and **"Think and Grow Rich"** by Napoleon Hill. Two of the best personal development, people skills, getting along with other people, attitude, and goal setting books ever written.

Please get basic paperback copies of each book right away. They are an integral part of implementing the ideas in this book.

Let's get started. There's never going to be a better time for me to help you BECOME BRAND NEW! This is a powerful road map that, when followed, will help you **STAND OUT, DOMINATE, and PROSPER!**

Chapter 1:

An UNBELIEVABLE Attitude

Most people, when trying to achieve greater success, don't realize that it's very important to work on having a great attitude every day. The main difference between "average" and those who "create exceptional outcomes" is ATTITUDE. **We alter our lives by altering our attitudes.**

Before making you a branding expert, I believe we have to work on your attitude, and make sure that you are a great example of what your brand represents.

Every day, when we wake up, we subconsciously choose an attitude, whether positive or negative. Unfortunately, it's easier to choose a negative attitude because that gives us the excuse to not take the important steps that can take our life to the next level.

Attitude is the way you see your life – your experiences, your opportunities, your challenges, your choices, and your responses. It is the direction that you move at any given moment. Your attitude either builds up your life or tears it down. Whether you're winning or losing is determined by your attitude. Losers see the loss of a job as the end of the road. Winners see an opportunity to find a better job or start a business of their own. Losers look at a rainy day and see their outdoor plans ruined. Winners see an opportunity to go singing in the rain. Winners embrace life with a wonderful positive attitude. Losers let life's challenges bring them down.

A great attitude begins with **a smile**. Even if you don't feel like it, fake it. It'll make you feel better. In fact, it takes fewer facial muscles to smile than it does to frown. Be a beacon of warm, positive feelings to others, and those rays of sunshine will come back to shine brightly on you. You will then attract people with a similar positive attitude. The difference between average people and those who are very successful is a positive attitude. **Champions choose to think and behave differently and now you do too.**

If an adversity strikes, get excited about finding the opportunity that exists in that situation. With an open, positive mind, solutions will come much quicker and you'll be proud of yourself for the way you responded.

Whatever we think about we become. Whatever the mind focuses on, it expands. Our present thoughts determine our future. A positive attitude makes it possible to create the future we desire. A negative attitude attracts difficulties, and is often responsible for bad health. Otherwise, how would you explain why some people's health fails quickly, when they believe that they only have a short time to live, while others survive and do very well even though they've been diagnosed with a so-called *terminal* illness?

If you need to improve your attitude, and thus get you on the road to creating exceptional outcomes, the following affirmations, declared the first thing each morning, and the last thing each night, will help:

EVERYTHING I TOUCH PROSPERS AND SUCCEEDS!

I'M AN EXPERT AT STANDING OUT, DOMINATING MY MARKET, AND PROSPERING!

I HAVE A GREAT, POSITIVE, CAN DO ATTITUDE.

I ATTRACT GREAT OPPORTUNITIES.

I AM CREATING MY EXCEPTIONAL OUTCOMES!

The goal is to create a card, about the size of a business card, upon which you will type a few of the most valuable affirmations that can help you create exceptional outcomes and make you a branding expert. In a following chapter, I'll relate what you'll do with that card to add further power to your life.

Don't analyze the affirmations. Just declare them with conviction. What you're doing is programming your powerful brain, which has more capabilities than the most powerful computer man could create. Most people program the computer between their ears with failure affirmations, and then they're surprised when things don't work out.

And, as you go about your day, people will periodically ask you, *"How's business?"* or *"How's everything?"* What you say next is really important and exhibits your brand, good or bad. Most people will tell you exactly how things are. That's not impressive and it's not memorable. Since I'm here to help you create exceptional outcomes, we want people to walk away thinking you're doing great. That way they will spread good rumors about you and bring great opportunities to you. People like dealing with people who exude confidence, and seem to be successful. They "brand" those people as being special!

If we need to, we're going to *FAKE IT TILL WE MAKE IT!* You see, we're either pretending things are getting better, or allowing them to stay the same. So, when people ask *"How's business?"* or *"How's everything?"* I suggest you respond enthusiastically with one word: ***UNBELIEVABLE!*** You're actually telling the truth. That will cover both ends of the spectrum, good or bad. But, when you do it with enthusiasm, most everyone will give you the benefit of the doubt and think you're doing great.

Then, when they ask, *"Is it really going that good?"* Answer by saying, *"All I can say is, it's UNBELIEVABLE! How's everything with you?"* Turn the conversation back to them. Do this with enthusiasm for 30 days and watch what happens. Guess who this process works the most on? YOU! People walk away smiling and you'll feel better about whatever is going on in your life at the moment.

I mentioned that when you say UNBELIEVABLE, you should do so with enthusiasm. There's another key to your creating exceptional outcomes and exuding a great brand – ***ENTHUSIASM!*** The word comes from the Greek language, meaning *"God within"*. It is the spark that top achievers harness and it helps them achieve great things. They have made a habit of bringing it to the forefront, whether they feel like it or not.

But, there are days when all of us don't feel like being enthusiastic. There are days when I don't feel like being enthusiastic. Perhaps the plane came in late the night before a presentation I was to make. Or maybe someone wasn't nice to me. For whatever reason, let's say I'm in a bad mood.

However, before I walk in to be in front of an audience, I've got to have an attitude adjustment. The first thing I do is realize that *attitude is everything*. Then I think about the fact that *the group runs at the speed of the leader*. Wait a minute. I am the leader this morning. They're going to run at my speed? This is not going to be good. Then I think about the following:

"A leader does what has to be done, when it has to be done, whether they feel like it or not."

One other thing I do to get myself in a better mood comes from my days as a television director. I remember being in a television studio in Los Angeles years ago, late at night, directing my television program. Everyone was tired. I, as the director, needed to get everyone's attitude up so we could get the show done and go home. Thus, on the headset in the control room, and to everyone in the TV studio, I said two words to get everyone's attitude up: **IT'S SHOWTIME!**

When I did that with enthusiasm, everyone's energy improved. All I had to do was keep up that "SHOWTIME" energy for a few minutes and, for the rest of the program, I was operating on the improved energy of everyone else.

However, what does the average person do? The average person will knock themselves out of the saddle before they get on the horse. Some say, *"I'm so tired. Nobody's nice to me. Things don't work out for me. I cannot create a dominant brand!"*

Even if we feel that way, expressing it to ourselves is counterproductive, and puts roadblocks in our own way. Thus, since I'm determined to help you create exceptional outcomes, and make you a branding expert, let's use the words **UNBELIEVABLE** and **IT'S SHOWTIME** in order to exude a great attitude.

John D. Rockefeller, the founder of the family fortune said that **"attitude is everything"**. It was not part of the thing, not a majority of the thing, it was everything! If you have the attitude that you could never create an exceptional brand, you're right. If you think you can, you're right. In other words, *whichever way you see anything, you're right*! It may not be good for you, but you're right.

Follow these concepts for 90 days, with ENTHUSIASM, and watch what happens. You'll be on your way to BECOMING BRAND NEW! And you will **STAND OUT, DOMINATE, and PROSPER!**

Chapter 2:
Identify Your "WHY"

It's really important for everyone to identify a reason to do better. According to Napoleon Hill, in the book ***"Think and Grow Rich,"*** it's vital to identify your next reward. Something you would do for yourself once you become a branding expert and achieve the next level of success.

When thinking about creating exceptional outcomes, most people are so concerned about the HOW, and not the WHY, that they never take that leap of faith that could change their whole life.

For example, if someone wants to become a great musician, they worry about the cost of lessons, the time it'll take to get good, how to get a break in the industry. That usually keeps them from taking any steps toward that dream. Instead, they should focus on the WHY. What if becoming a great musician has been a passion their entire life? Something that must be accomplished. *They've gotta have it!* That's a powerful WHY. **When the WHY is exciting enough, the HOW doesn't matter**. In our example, if that person focused regularly on their passion for music, the WHY, and take action, the HOW would take care of itself.

Here's another example: Let's say your daughter is two

years old and she's asleep in the bedroom. You're in the living room. You smell smoke and see it coming out from under her door. Your daughter starts crying. You're not a large person and the door is locked. Is there any question about the HOW? No. You're crashing through that door to save your daughter because the WHY is big enough.

The average person will sit there and think about the HOW. They'll think about the fact that the door is made of solid wood. And it has one of those heavy-duty locks. I know that's an exaggeration. But is it? Most people will deliberate about the HOW until it's too late. Not you. You are now focusing on your WHY.

The WHY in your life has to be something exciting, something FOR YOU. It cannot be food, shelter or clothing. Your subconscious mind will only get excited about something that includes a reward for you. It doesn't mean you shouldn't take care of your family. It simply means that you will be passionate about something that includes an exciting reward for YOU.

If travel is your WHY, your passion, identify where you want to go and get pictures of that destination. If it's a specific new vehicle, get pictures of you sitting in that vehicle. If it's a new house, find one you desire and take pictures of you and your family in front of that house. Post those pictures where you can see them every day. ***Keep your WHY constantly in front of you and you'll figure out the HOW.***

Helen Keller said that *"life is either a great adventure or it is nothing."* Unfortunately, most people live a life of quiet desperation. Not you. You are reading this book because you want to transform your life. You're looking for direction, for something that you can get passionate about. If you don't have a WHY identified, please read this affirmation: *It's* (set a date three months from now) _____. *I've discovered my burning desire and I'm excited.* This is an affirmation that will harness the power of your subconscious mind, in order to identify your WHY.

If, by the date set, you have still not discovered your WHY, reset the date for another three months in the future. One day, it'll suddenly come to you. And the rest will be history.

Most people focus on the HOW rather than the WHY. The HOW is the process and the WHY is the reason. The HOW deals with "How do I make enough money? How do I save money? How do I get ahead?" Making money for food, shelter, and clothing is important, but not exciting.

The WHY deals with rewards along the way. Without rewards, the mind can get tired and depressed. In the final analysis, we all, sooner or later, say, *"What's in it for me?"* When you reward yourself, you'll be better to everyone around you.

When the WHY is exciting enough, the HOW doesn't matter! Get a picture of your next WHY and put that picture on the back side of the card that contains your affirmations. Then have that card laminated, perhaps at a FedEx Office location, and look at the card the first thing each morning and the last thing each night. Declare your affirmations and look at the picture. Watch what happens in the next few months!

Some important thoughts from author Darwin P. Kinglsey: ***"You have powers you never dreamed of. You can do things you never thought you could do. There are no limitations in what you can do except the limitations in your own mind as to what you cannot do. Don't think you cannot. Think you can."***

You don't have to be born with a silver spoon in your mouth to be successful, to have a lot of money, or the right connections. As Napoleon Hill stated in the book ***Think and Grow Rich***, you have to **"clearly define, in writing, what you want, develop a plan to get it, and get started. Then establish a reward."** With that type of *"definiteness of purpose"*, and the series of concepts I'm sharing here, you'll be ready to take branding to a whole new level. You will **STAND OUT, DOMINATE, and PROSPER!**

Chapter 3:
Your Daily Success Formula

By now you should have produced your laminated goals card with a few specific affirmations on one side, and a picture of your next reward on the other side. If you haven't done that yet, please stop and do it now. It's an important part of the process to help you become an expert at branding.

If you have produced your goals card, then let's proceed to a Daily Success Formula that will ensure that you'll be in a great, positive mood, to start every day. Of the many CEOs that I have spoken before over the years, I came to realize that the most successful ones worked on their attitude on a daily basis. They realized, as I noted before, that *attitude is everything*.

The following formula is a simple way for you to focus on a great attitude every day. It is a simple and powerful process to transform your life, and help you create exceptional outcomes.

You, your family, your goals, and your success are very important to me. In my over 30 years of experience as a consultant and professional speaker, I've conducted extensive research into why some people do very well in life and others do not. The key, I discovered, was the repetition of certain simple and valuable habits, over and over and over.

The following Daily Success Formula is simple, easy to implement, and most of it takes less than eight minutes a day.

It will help you solve your challenges, make your work easier, help you with your personal relationships, energize your future and lead you toward prosperity. These are the six simple steps of the formula:

1. Affirmations

2. The 30-Day Prosperity Plan

3. Readings

4. Exercises

5. The Fortune Fund

6. Action

Step 1 is Affirmations. As noted before, these are statements of things you desire, written as if they were already accomplished. By now you should have already formulated your affirmations, and started reading them, out loud, the first thing every morning, and the last thing each night.

Step 2 is called *The 30-Day Prosperity Plan.* Most people wake up each morning either listening to the radio, reading the newspaper, or watching television news, while getting ready for the day. The majority of information that we get from those three mediums is negative.

If you had just purchased a new living room carpet, would you allow a neighbor to come over and dump garbage on it? Of course not. What about your mind? You've just had a restful night's sleep. Your mind is nice and clean. You turn on the radio, read the paper, or watch television in the morning, and they dump a bunch of negative news right into your nice clean mind. If you wouldn't let a neighbor dump garbage onto your new living room carpet, why would you let someone dump negative news into your nice clean mind?

What we do first thing in the morning sets the tone for our entire day. In fact, *the first 15 minutes of our day set the mood for our entire day*.

Instead of turning on the radio, reading the paper, or watching television, why not put on a positive audio CD or a positive program on your computer? Put a CD player on the counter in the bathroom, insert a motivating positive audio message, and listen to it while getting ready in the morning. Just two or three minutes. The next day do the same. Listen to the same CD or program over and over and over, for months. Repetition is the mother of skill. Soon, the positive thoughts that you are hearing, and repeating every morning, will become a part of you, and they will help build your confidence.

Step 3 is Readings. While positive audio CDs build motivation, reading builds character. Listening to audio CD's is *someone else talking to you*. Reading is *you talking to you*.

I strongly suggest, as I mentioned earlier, that you immediately purchase a copy of *How to Win Friends and Influence People* by Dale Carnegie, and *Think and Grow Rich* by Napoleon Hill. These books will give you the right words you need to communicate successfully with people, and will build your confidence to an above-average level.

A key to success, which I discovered in my research, deals with reading. The average person reads no more than two non-fiction books from the time they get out of school until the time they die. Of those people who do read personal development books, one after another, they usually do not internalize any of them. *Reading a book once does nothing.* That goes in one ear and out the other. Repetition, as noted, is the mother of skill. Thus, my recommendation is to read just two books, over and over and over.

The two chosen, ***How to Win Friends and Influence People*** and ***Think and Grow Rich***, were both written many years ago, and have been great resources for success for tens of thousands of people worldwide. They are still both applicable today.

How to Win Friends and Influence People is one of the all-time bestselling books in the field of personal development. It contains many common sense ideas that can help all of us to better get along with others at work, with our families, and with friends. It reminds us of many common courtesies that most people miss most of the time. In my opinion, it has been, and still is today, the finest manual available in dealing with other people. Your ability in dealing with people will greatly determine how strong a brand you develop.

Think and Grow Rich is the book which has made more millionaires than any other book in history. In my opinion, it is the best book around in teaching us how to deal with *ourselves,* and our attitude toward success. This is a very valuable book from the standpoint of simple ideas that deal with goal-setting, success, money, and prosperity. It's basically an attitude book.

Once you've purchased the two books, start reading just one page a day in each. When you complete the books, start over again. Read these books over and over and over, until the valuable thoughts in them become a part of you. These books will give you the right words, and the confidence to help you achieve your goals.

Let me re-emphasize the importance of this simple, daily reading process in these two particular books. The purpose for the continued repetition of the reading of these two books is that, once thoroughly internalized, the principles in them will bring you more happiness and success than 98% of the world's people will ever experience!

The first time through you will probably want to underline anything that seems important to you in each book. Later, in other readings of the same material, other thoughts may come to mind, and may need to be underlined.

Take the two books with you when you leave the house. Often there are moments when you're waiting. Use that time to read. If you have a challenging moment during the day, open one of the two books, and read for a couple of minutes. This habit will change gears for you. Being upset is like playing with poison. You need to get rid of it quickly. Otherwise, you could infect everyone around you. Use these books to diffuse difficult moments.

Thus, your immediate assignment for today is to purchase the two books, and begin reading just one page a day in each. You will begin seeing positive changes in your attitude and in your life, within the next few days, and steadily thereafter.

I felt that these two books were so valuable that, years ago, I read each book, once a month, every month, for 5 years. I read both of those books 60 times each! Now they are a part of me.

Step 4 is Exercise. I almost died three times in my life. I'm fine now. But now I exercise at least three times each week. Not because I have to, but because I can, and I want to continue to have good health.

Regular exercise keeps our bodies toned, and stimulates good health. At the same time, it is a great tension reliever. When we get a good cardio-vascular workout, that stimulates the brain in a positive way. It increases productivity and stimulates creativity.

So, if you haven't exercised regularly for quite a while, that's OK. Let's get started somewhere. How about a five minute walk in your neighborhood, three times a week? Start there and then gradually increase to 30 minutes, three times a week. Maybe you can call a friend and walk together. Do something. Do it today. Don't be like a friend of mine. His idea of exercise was to fill the tub, pull the plug, and fight the current.

Step 5 is the Fortune Fund. I assume that one of your main objectives in pursuing your goals is to increase your income, and reach a point of financial independence. The *Fortune Fund* is a powerful tool to help accomplish that dream. It is a simple and systematic program of daily savings.

The main aim of this step in the success formula is to raise your money consciousness to a higher level. Unfortunately, most people find it difficult to save money and thus accumulate their fortune. One reason is that when the idea of savings comes up, if at any time, it's only once each month. Some people save through a payroll deduction program while others try to make savings a part of their monthly budget. The budget idea doesn't work well because there usually isn't much left over at the end of each month.

Throughout every year a considerable amount of money passes by each of us. The aim of the *Fortune Fund* is to stop some of that money and redirect it toward a special place. It will go into a fund that is never to be touched. This fund will become a confidence builder as well as a form of security for extreme emergencies. Most tasks in life are easier to accomplish if we know that we have some money in the bank to back us.

So, the *Fortune Fund* has been developed as an easy way to begin a savings habit. Since the subconscious mind cannot tell the difference between a one-dollar bill and a thousand-dollar bill, saving a little bit of money each day works great to raise your money consciousness.

Get an envelope, label it *My Fortune Fund*, and put at least a dollar in it every day. If you have a little extra, deposit a little more. As you put the paper money in the envelope (paper money seems to have a greater impact on the mind than coins), say the following phrase:

I'm richer today than I was yesterday. Not as rich as I'll be tomorrow.

The idea is that something is being saved every day. The main point is that your mind sees something tangible building because of all your efforts. You are literally becoming richer every day as a result of everything you are doing.

When you have enough in the envelope to open a savings account at a nearby bank, do so. Ask for a passbook. Continue making the daily deposits in your envelope. Then, once a week, deposit the money in the envelope into your savings account, and note the deposit in your passbook.

The reason for the passbook is that you will see the amount changing and your fortune growing every week. After each weekly deposit at the bank, look at the entries in your passbook and make a mental impression. As your mind sees the progressively growing column of positive numbers, it will be noting the fact that you really are richer today than you were yesterday. And that you are richer this week than you were last week. And that all of your efforts are making this happen. This is a powerful form of motivation!

Once the *Fortune Fund* begins to grow, most people get excited about the progress and want to deposit even more into the account. Thus, one reason for a greater urgency to move on with your goals. This money is not to be touched. It is your permanent *Fortune Fund* and it will give you an incredible money consciousness.

If you are heavily in debt, STOP whatever you're doing that continues that trend. Stop using credit cards for impulse buying and focus on becoming debt free. If you owe several debts, make minimum payments to all of them, and focus on getting rid of the smallest one first. That will give you momentum. Then focus on the next one, and so on.

Step 6 is Action. Take some kind of action every day on your most important goals. Just doing this formula, on a daily basis, is action.

Your affirmations, properly broken down, will help you define the action steps that you can take each day. The greatest antidote to fear is ACTION, ACTION, ACTION.

Let's analyze how much time I'm suggesting that you spend on the formula each day. Reading your affirmations in the morning and in the evening should take no more than a couple of minutes. You can listen to a positive audio CD when you're getting ready in the morning. Reading one page a day in the Carnegie and Hill books should only take a few minutes. Your exercise program can begin with five minutes, three times a week. Putting a dollar bill in your *Fortune Fund* envelope should only take a few seconds. Concerning the *Action* step, you just took some action by doing the formula.

An added benefit to doing the formula every day is the discipline that it develops in you. Small agreements lead to large agreements. When you make a small agreement with yourself to do the formula on a regular basis, that is the foundation for developing larger agreements. Productive small habits lead to lucrative larger habits. Most successful people have become that way because of the valuable habits they developed and followed.

This Daily Success Formula is a result of many years of studying the habits of successful people. Now you are going to follow the very same path. Is there any question about the results? Not in my mind.

You are unique. You are special. You are destined for greatness. This formula is a powerful vehicle to carry you there! And, it will help you become BRAND NEW!

Years ago I ran my own advertising agency for 10 years. Combining that experience, along with nearly 20 years of sharing marking ideas with over 25,000 CEO's worldwide, I've assembled a list of very productive branding and marketing ideas. Some of these have generated millions of dollars in profits for the executives who used them. None of them cost much money.

This book is a compilation of the best ideas dealing with attitude, success, and branding that I developed and tested over many years. It is clearly intended to help you **STAND OUT, DOMINATE, and PROSPER!**

Chapter 4:
Habits of Successful People

As you may be noticing, I feel it's really important to combine a great attitude, positive thinking, and great branding ideas in order to become a leader in your field. For many years, I have studied the habits of successful people and want to share with you some observations.

Successful people got that way by following certain high-achievement habits. They have identified in writing exactly what they want out of life, they want it passionately, and they formulate a plan to get it.

Successful people often find themselves in leadership positions because they know the value of being great communicators. They are constantly looking for opportunities to get up and speak in front of people. Dale Carnegie, in the book *How to Win Friends and Influence People,* said that the ability to speak in front of people is a shortcut to distinction. If you need improvement in this area, check into the Dale Carnegie course in your city. It is well worth the investment!

In addition to being focused, and being great communicators, successful people know that money is first made in their minds. They see themselves in possession of large sums of money ahead of its appearance. They also know that some of everything they earn is theirs to keep. They pay themselves first, with at least 10% of their income, and then they get their money to work for them. Your reading of the book **Think and Grow Rich** will help you think the same way.

Successful people also treat their money with great respect. The pay in cash whenever possible, stay out of debt, and they don't mind saving for something special. They realize that if they take care of the small money, they will eventually have large money. And that money, one day, will take care of them.

Successful people also create powerful relationships with successful, positive people who encourage each other. Successful people know that time is valuable. They prioritize the five most valuable tasks each day, and go after them with passion. Successful people seize opportunities.

Successful people are great communicators. Showing genuine interest in other people makes them feel important. And, by letting the other person do most of the talking, while they listen, they're considered great communicators.

Successful people don't sweat the small stuff. They handle stress differently. They know that it's not what happens, it's how we react to the things that happen. They react calmly and decisively. Persistence plays a big part in the lives of successful people. They stick to something they're passionate about until they reach their desired goal. And, when action is needed, successful people take immediate action. They know that ***he who hesitates, falters***.

Successful people have a positive attitude. They expect good things to happen. By doing the *Daily Success Formula,* you now think like a successful person and good things are coming into your life.

Successful people understand that *reading builds character*. With the right books, it puts the right words in our minds. I suggest you get copies of the Carnegie and Hill books for everyone in your company, and ask them to keep them on their desks. ***What we focus on, expands!***

Following the habits of successful people could help you be different, act differently, prosper differently, **STAND OUT, DOMINATE, and PROSPER!**

Chapter 5:
Creating Your USP

When it comes to branding, most companies have no memorable, productive USP. That stands for a Unique Selling Proposition. It's a short phrase that stops people in their tracks when they ask you what you do. The aim is to get people to pay total attention for a few seconds so that they might tell others about your company.

You know some USP's. What company says "We bring good things to life?" That's GE – General Electric. Our aim is to literally hire a bunch of people to be your sales people without paying them a penny. Most people make the mistake of creating a catchy slogan that everyone at their company likes. If your people like your slogan, it's probably not a good USP. The whole purpose is to brand you as being unique and memorable!

The aim, when you give someone a strong USP, is for them to be stopped in their tracks and for them to say, "What are you talking about?" Then we've got their attention. Everyone's mind runs at about 1,500 words a minute. We've got seconds to stop that pattern and make an impression that will last a long time. Then they might tell others about you and you'll get a call out of nowhere stating, "Someone was telling me about you."

From my research with over 25,000 CEO's, I found that a good USP should be:

1. **Short** – the GE USP is 6 words. Any longer than that, in my opinion, is too long and all people will remember is the last word.

2. **Not Logical** – "We make widgets. We build busses." These are too logical and easy to forget.

3. **Start with the word "We"** – this makes it sound as if humans are involved. It's not just a building somewhere. Also, "We" sounds larger. "I" sounds small.

4. **Include the word "You"** - I was taught in marketing classes in college that when you include the word "You" in any form of marketing or advertising, you get me involved. You're talking directly to me and not to the masses.

Thus, the template we want to fill in, in order to get you a strong brand, is:

We do _____ for you.

Let me give you some examples.

Plumbing Company
   We're the pipeline of your dreams.

Home Builder
   We bring your dreams home.

Staffing Company
   We people your success.

Financial Services
   We watch your tomorrows.

Paint Company
   We color your world beautifully.

Car Dealership
We're big wheels in your life.

Travel Agency
We take you where you've wanted.

Insurance Agency
We protect what concerns you.

Architectural Firm
We'll floor you with our ideas.

Commercial Builder
We're the pillars of your future.

You might get your employees to help you come up with a good USP. However, it's imperative that they use the template "We do _____ for you." Conduct a contest among your employees and put up some nice prizes. That will make them feel important. Google your potential USP choices and see if anyone is using them. Even if they are, as long as it's in another industry, and there would be no confusion, you can get it trademarked for your company. Do so with a good trademark attorney.

Your USP should then be on everything - website, business cards, all advertising, and it should be used when your receptionist answers your phone. It should also be in the signature portion of all emails you send with the "TM" trademark notation in smaller type. This will make your emails more impressive. People will give you credit for being a bigger company.

There are marketing and advertising agencies in major cities that charge companies hundreds of thousands of dollars to create a USP. Using the process I've described, you could do the same thing without spending much money. Start observing and you'll see where major companies could have made a bigger branding impact by making some slight changes in their USP.

For example, the USP for Chevrolet is "Find New Roads". May I ask, *whose roads*? They could be talking to anyone. How about "*We find your new roads*?" Now they would be talking to ME. The GE USP above is "*We bring good things to life.*" What if that was changed to "*We bring good things to your life*?" Now they would be talking to me.

Good branding stops people in their tracks and makes a strong impression that will get you more business. Let's make sure that your branding is strong and memorable when people ask "*What do you do?*" A strong USP will help you **STAND OUT, DOMINATE, and PROSPER!**

Chapter 6:
Branding in Texts & Emails

Most people lose great branding opportunities in the texts and emails they send every day. Great branding is a series of impressions that all make an impact – good or bad. It's a series of small steps that, when taken cumulatively, either give someone a strong, positive impression, or no impression at all.

Concerning texts, unless it's to a family member or friend, ALWAYS include their first name and your first name. Ever get a text from someone that simply says, "See you at the meeting in 3 weeks." WHO, WHAT, WHERE? I'm supposed to guess, out of almost 8 billion people on earth, who this person is? Not much puts me in a bad mood. That puts me in a bad mood. I have to text back and, apologetically, ask "Who is this?"

But, then, it's not their fault. It's mine. I thought maybe they'd read the Dale Carnegie book, "How to Win Friends and Influence People." Apparently they had not. Carnegie said, "To each of us, the most important thing in life is our name. It is the sweetest sound in any language."

What if I send a text, with no names, to a prospective client? What if that omission turns them off and I don't even know what happened? I don't want you to lose any branding opportunities. In business matters, please take the time to be clear in all texts. Include their first name and yours and give any details that would clarify who you are.

Concerning emails, I always address people by their name in EVERY EMAIL I send out each day, even if it's a series of emails to the same person in one day. Ever get an email from someone and they just start talking? They don't address you by name. I look at the top of the email to see if it was addressed to me because, in reality, it was not addressed to me. They didn't greet me by name. I would rather be accused of being overly-courteous than having no manners at all.

And, if you're sending a series of emails to one person on a given day, change the subject line so they can go back to an important point without having to read all of the emails again.

The signature portion of your emails is another great branding opportunity that most people miss completely. These days, signatures on emails look like an afterthought. Usually just a name, as if this person's name ought to be recognized easily by everyone. Not so. Let's make sure that the signature on all your emails exemplifies strong branding on your part. Here are the essential items I suggest:

1. Your full name

2. Your full address

3. *(If it's to one of your 10 most valuable clients)* Your cell phone number

4. Your USP with the letters "TM" once it's trademarked

5. Your picture

Having your address in your signature makes you look like a real business. What if I want to visit the company and buy something? What if you're in a distant city, and I will be there for a meeting? I might want to come by. One CEO told me how important an address in the email signature is. Her company was bidding against nine other companies for a big deal. They got the big deal.

The CEO of the new client company took her aside afterward and told her something very important. He said, "Let me tell what we liked about your company from the beginning that was different than the other nine companies trying to get our business. All the emails we got from your company had your street address in the signatures. None of the other nine companies had their street address in the signatures. You were the only one who looked like a real business. All I can do is share with you this information. Was the street address in the winning company's signature valuable? The CEO told me it was eventually worth over a million dollars!

Concerning your phone number in the signature of your emails, make sure that it's easy for people to call you. Have a direct number at work rather than one with extensions. If I have to go through someone's telephone jungle to reach them, I might eventually want to hunt in someone else's jungle. If you're writing to one of your ten most valuable clients, be sure to list your cell phone number. If I'm one of your important clients, and I would rather talk on the phone about an email than write back, it would give me great confidence if I could reach you easily.

Adding your picture, a recent headshot rather than a kindergarten picture, is a personal touch that further enhances your branding. We all meet a lot of people these days. How in the world can we keep track of everyone? Thus, seeing your picture, may jog their memory and get them to connect better with you. "Oh, that's who he is. Oh, I remember her from that meeting." I have my picture in the signature of all of my emails. People often tell me, "Boaz, I like getting your emails because I get to see your smiling face."

Have the IT people at your company create your email signature as a unit – address, phone number, USP, and picture. You don't want the picture to be an attachment, which could make people think it's a virus. I suggest that the entire signature unit be prepared so it comes up every time you write an email.

You want to be unique and different with your branding? Complete texts and emails will help you do that because the majority of people will not think this is that important. Let them think that, while you move ahead, and pass them on the road to greater success! You are about to **STAND OUT, DOMINATE, and PROSPER!**

Chapter 7:
Branding Through the Media

Call the media, both local and national, and tell them that you're sick and tired of hearing all of the negative stories about business. Your company is doing great and you think they ought to come out and do a story on you. What if someone says, "Yes"?

When I was in college, I used to work on the assignment desk of a television station in the Midwest. Our job was to find stories and to send our reporters out to cover those stories. If you call an assignment editor at a television station, you're helping them do their job! They're looking for stories to cover every day.

Call the local television stations, radio stations, newspapers, and the business journal in your area. Tell them that your company is very successful, and that you think they should come out and interview you. Again, what if someone says *"Yes"*? You might even contact national TV networks, such as CNN, and see what happens.

Someone in one of my audiences did call CNN. They came out, did a feature on his company, and ran it on CNN Worldwide. He now puts that in the signature of all of his emails: *As featured on CNN Worldwide*. I believe that it's all perception when it comes to success.

Another audience member, going through a tough economic time in Chicago with his office remodeling company, called the biggest paper in town, told them his company was doing great, and they did a big feature, with pictures, about his company. That article, and the positive reactions from the community, kept his company from going broke!

Look at your industry and identify a trend that might be interesting to the general public. Do as much research on that trend as possible, and make notes of valuable resources. Call the major television networks and tell them that, when they need an expert dealing with your topic, you would be available. Send hand-written note cards as a follow-up, with your business card, again expressing your willingness to be called on at any time as an on-air expert.

Once you do one of these for one network, you might let the other networks know that people now value your expertise. Just making a few of these appearances can greatly enhance your branding. People want to deal with someone they consider an expert.

You could do the same thing with your local television stations. Do enough research to find information about your industry that might be constantly updated, perhaps quarterly? Offer to be a non-paid reporter for them, giving the quarterly results of your research. Again, your information has to be of interest to the general public.

After one or two of these appearances, you could then say to prospective clients, *You may have seen me on television locally and sometimes nationally*. That's very impressive. Put these clips on your YouTube Channel.

This is a great way to brand yourself successful, **STAND OUT, DOMINATE, and PROSPER!**

Chapter 8:
Brand This Idea "The FedEx"

From my time in owning my own advertising agency, I find that great branding and outstanding marketing don't result from sending out 300 emails over a period of weeks. I find that it's much more productive to focus on 10 clients you really want, and do a strong, consistent campaign to them.

The following is an 11-week campaign to 10 specific companies you want as clients. In my many audiences of CEO's over many years, I've never seen someone do the entire 11-week campaign and not get a new client. So, here is the process...

Identify the 10 companies that you would like to have as clients, your ideal list. Identify the CEO of each of those companies. My mother, who was a great people-person, told me to start with the top. Send a one-page, hand-written letter, to each of those CEO's, stating why your company and your services could be of benefit to them, and that you would like to set up a meeting for coffee:

"With our expertise at X, Y, and Z, I think we could be of service to your company and I'd like to set up a meeting for coffee".

If your handwriting is sloppy, slow down. Would you rather

be stuck with 200 emails that never get answered? Attach your business card to the letter. They might want to call you.

Tell me this, haven't the folks at FedEx sold us on the idea that, if it comes in a FedEx overnight envelope, it's got to be important. People pay attention to these envelopes. And, isn't that what strong branding is all about?

Send these letters once a week, every week, same day, by FedEx, until they call or issue a restraining order. Even then, you could say, "Before we go to court, could we meet?" Just kidding. Maybe not. You could send these letters on a Wednesday for third-day delivery. They will show up Monday morning. They won't know it's not overnight, and you'll save some money.

The fourth week, for those who haven't responded, add some yellow Post-It Notes, hand written, on top of the hand-written letters. One could say, *"I'm sure glad you finally opened this."* Another could say, *"Aren't you impressed with how I got your attention?"*

A company in California, whose CEO attended one of my seminars, told me they had been trying to get into the door of a big company, WD-40, for five years. They did my FedEx campaign and, after the fourth week, they got a call from the Vice President of WD-40. He said, *"I don't know what you did to my CEO, but he told me to call you."*

So, tell me, is it better to continue going after someone in conventional ways for five years or better to use this FedEx campaign and get them *to call you in four weeks?*

On the seventh week, to those who've not responded, send a new baseball in a little box, by FedEx, with the following Post-It Note: *"I'm the one sending the Monday morning FedEx*

letters. Sooner or later we will play ball. So give me a call."
Instead, you may choose to send a basketball by FedEx. Use a magic marker to write on it *"Give us a shot."* One audience member, in the seventh week of the FedEx campaign, got a call from the CEO of a billion-dollar corporation who thought he was silly and invited him over. That turned into a **$5-million-dollar profit over the next two years!**

One CEO in the Northeast, who had been to one of my seminars, and came up with the basketball instead of the baseball in the seventh week, told me that he got several new clients using this process. He further related that, when he walked into the offices of the CEO's of the new client companies, they all had his basketball on their credenzas. That's what I call strong branding!

In the tenth week, for those who have not responded, call their secretary and find out their shoe size. Then send one brand new shoe in a box with the following note:

"I'm the one sending the Monday morning FedExes. Now that I've got one foot in the door, call me."

In the eleventh week, for those who haven't responded, send the matching shoe with the note:

"I'm the one sending the Monday morning FedExes. I know what you were waiting for to call me. You were waiting for the other shoe to drop. It just did."

I have found that it's much more productive to do a creative campaign to 10 valuable potential clients, for 11 weeks, and get some of them, rather than do a three-week email campaign to a 100 potential clients and get nothing. People tell me that they're getting into huge companies using this idea. What have you got to lose?

A CEO, in a group in St. Louis, who runs a big insurance company, told me that they got 10 new clients using my FedEx idea. Another CEO, in the same group, told me that they had been trying to get into the door of Ford Motor Company for several years. They did my FedEx campaign and got into Ford in 5 weeks!

In the weeks that I haven't made a specific suggestion, be creative. A one-minute video, personalized to each CEO, could go something like this: "Hi, _____. I'm _____. I'm the one sending the Monday morning FedExes. I thought you might want to see that I'm a really nice guy. Have a great day." I'm all about shaking people up. I want them to think about YOU!

Some people think that my FedEx idea is silly, old, and corny. Let me ask you this: If a silly, old, corny idea could bring your company an extra million dollars, would you be open to that idea? I believe most people would respond positively. What have you got to lose?

If you're not doing something bold in your branding, you could be left behind. The FedEx campaign makes you **STAND OUT, DOMINATE, and PROSPER!**

Chapter 9:
Voicemail into Commercials

Your voicemail is another touch point at which people experience your brand. What kind of impression is your voicemail making when people call and they get your recording? Most people's voicemail messages sound like they've already died, and we should have buried them an hour ago.

Change your voicemail and turn it into a commercial. Let's make your voice message, and that of everyone in your company, work for you by promoting what you do. To make you different, leave a message such as the following:

"This is John. I'm busy helping a client (make more money, get more sales, etc.). Leave a message and I'll call you back so we can do the same for you." Show everyone that you are different.

If you're traveling for business, leave the following message:

"This is _____. I'm sorry I missed your call. I'm in Miami today helping a client take his company to the next level. Please leave a message so I can call you back, and we can do the same thing for your company."

Change your voicemail every couple of weeks. Thus, when people call regularly, they'll get the impression that you are very busy, doing valuable things for clients. Isn't that what they want, someone who is in demand, doing valuable things for clients?

By the way, it's really important that you show enthusiasm on your phone message and when you answer the phone. Napoleon Hill, in the book "Think and Grow Rich", said that enthusiasm is a shortcut to your greater success. And, if you don't know how to be enthusiastic, just walk and talk 10% faster. No one will know what you're up to, but they'll like it.

And, for your 10 most valuable customers, and prospects, program their name and number into your phone. Then, when people call, you'll see their name come up on the screen on your phone. Greet them, with animation, using their name: *"John, I'm so glad you called me back."* This gives people a much warmer feeling and you're making them feel important by using the most important thing we have in life – **our name**.

This is an idea you can apply in the next 60 seconds. Please change your voicemail right now and state something you're doing for a client that's beneficial. Then add, *"And we can do the same thing for you. Leave a number."*

I got an email the other day from a CEO who adopted this idea across his whole company, 20 people. Some thought, initially, that the idea was corny. However, they all implemented it, and soon they started getting positive responses from many customers on their voicemail!! Is this making them stand out? Absolutely!

Changing your voicemail message on a regular basis is another important touch point that will help you **STAND OUT, DOMINATE, and PROSPER!**

Chapter 10:
The Client Brainstorm

I think we should all be treating our 10 most valuable clients with kid gloves. Because, if we don't, they may go somewhere else. Our strong branding ideas are going to help you keep those 10 clients and get more. The Client Brainstorm is a strong way to solidify your relationships with your 10 most valuable clients, and get them to go out and get more business for you! Here's how this idea works:

Call together the CEO's of your top 10 clients to a meeting at your office. If someone is at a distance, do a video hookup. If anyone competes with someone else in the group, hold two separate meetings. I don't want anyone to be uncomfortable.

Tell everyone how important they are to your company and how much you appreciate their business. After all, appreciation is the core of great relationships. When is the last time they ever got called to a meeting like this? In most cases, never.

Then tell them that, because they are so important to you, you want to share some powerful marketing ideas with them that you believe could help them get more business. You would begin by sharing the marketing ideas I'm sharing with you in this book. Just don't tell them the ideas are from me. I want you to get total credit. Hold another meeting three months later to see how your clients used the ideas.

Dale Carnegie relates that **"people are as interested in me as I am in them**." If any of your clients benefit from any of these ideas, human nature tells me that they'll look for ways to help you get more business. Tell me this, if one of your most important clients uses one of the branding and marketing ideas you share with them, and makes more money, guess who they will be grateful to forever? YOU!

That's what strong branding is all about. Making you stand out from everyone else. This idea certainly does that!

I can assure you, from my experience, that your competition will never think of this idea and, if they do hear about it, they won't take any action. That's why we're about to leave them in our dust!

We're here to take every step to make you different! Let's do more for your clients than they ever expected! Let's **STAND OUT, DOMINATE, and PROSPER!**

Chapter 11:
The Employee Brainstorm

If you're running a company, or a sales team, please realize that the employees who report to you can be a great resource for branding and marketing. Someone in accounting, who may seem like a quiet person, could have a great idea if we simply gave them the opportunity to express that idea. This could be part of a weekly company meeting.

I suggest that you call together all of your employees each week for a Monday morning 29-minute update. Tell them how important they are to your company and tell them that you need their help. Say the following:

"I need your help. If you were running this company, how would you lower expenses, improve productivity, keep current clients, or get more clients?" Also relate to them, *"If you don't have an idea, that's no problem."*

Don't ask for volunteers. Just start on one side of the room or the other, and call on each individual person by name. Make a big deal about any ideas that turn into productive action steps.

In order to set the best mood possible for these meetings, as a show of respect, start referring to your employees as *"Ladies and Gentleman"*. Also, at these meetings, go over what didn't work last week, and minimize it, while going over what did work and maximize that.

Dale Carnegie, in the book "How to Win Friends and Influence People" said, *"I will look for the good and embellish it* (make it bigger) *and, as much as possible, disregard the bad."* That doesn't mean we totally disregard the bad, but let's not beat a dead horse. Let's just not make it the whole program. Here is the warning from Carnegie: **"Whatever we focus on, expands!"** Go over what didn't work, and let people know what you're doing about it. Then, get excited and go over what did work so your people can get excited about that.

Monday morning is also a great time to introduce new team members. How often, in a new company, does someone come to work and, six months later, a lot of people still don't know that person? And, we wonder one day, "Why did they leave?" Maybe it was because we didn't make them feel important.

Dale Carnegie said, **"People need to feel important. They will do more for a feeling of importance than they will do for money."** I'm thinking that, if I throw enough money at a situation, surely a certain person will like me. Not if I make them feel small. They'll go somewhere else where people will make them feel important, even if the pay is a little less.

I got the following brilliant idea from a CEO in one of my audiences. On the first day of a new employee hire, he has the IT people create a bunch of poster boards with the new employee's picture and the following words: *"It's John Smith Day at XYZ Corporation. Welcome to our team."*

Then, he has people put up these poster boards at every entryway to his plant. Where everyone can see them when they come to work that day. "Did you see what they did for me? They made big posters and declared it my day!"

At lunch time, they throw a big ice cream social in the lunchroom in honor of that new team member. Everybody loves this, and it makes the new employee feel important. At the end of that first day, the CEO related, all of the employees stand on either side of a long hallway. The new employee is then "High-Fived" by everyone on his way home.

Tell me this, how much goodwill did they buy with that new employee on their first day? About a million-dollars-worth! Then, one day, if they need extra help, I would wager that this new employee will come to their rescue. Why? Because they made that person feel important from their first day.

These are strong branding ideas you can use with your employees. After all, they are your most important assets. Make them feel important and they will help you **STAND OUT, DOMINATE, and PROSPER!**

Chapter 12:
The Z-Card Phenomenon

Your business card is another branding touch point that most people miss. Too many business cards these days don't show an address of the business. As noted in Chapter 5 on Texts and Emails, showing an address makes the company look like a real business. Most business cards have no intrigue and do not generate further interest.

Entering stage left is truly a phenomenon. It's a business card, brochure, and website combination, that can tell your company's story in a very powerful way. It's called a Z-Card, perhaps for the unique way this large format presentation folds down to the size of a thick business card.

Thus, when folded up, the front cover looks exactly like your regular business card. It might be a good idea for you to go online right now and see what I'm talking about. Please go to ZCardNA.com.

Z-Cards come in different sizes. One size, I believe, is 8 ½ x 17. Since the printing is on both front and back, your Z-Card can be an abbreviated version of your website. It can contain pictures and descriptions of your products or services, testimonials from various clients, a how-to article, or whatever you feel would tell your story well and show great value in what you can do for people. Whatever would brand you as a leader in your field.

Most business cards either end up in a pile or get tossed away. The Z-Card is a handy, compact, powerful marketing tool, that is very effective in getting your message into the hands of potential customers. It was originally developed in Great Britain. In addition to going onto their website, if you wish to call, their North American headquarters is in New York City. Their number is 212-797-3450. If you call, ask for Tim. He's their North American President. He knows me. Tell him Boaz suggested you call. That won't get you anywhere, but it will sound impressive.

They have produced Z-Cards for American Airlines, Toyota, Mercedes Benz, and Disneyland. Since they've been around for many years, they've produced these cards for many different types of industries. Tell them what you do, and ask if they have any samples of companies in your field. They will send you those samples. If you wish to have one produced for yourself, they have a graphic department in New York to help with the designing of your Z-Card.

I have had my own Z-Card for a few years and have found that people don't toss them away. They are so beautifully done, with high quality paper, and they fold to open and close so beautifully, that people keep them for a long time. Let me see, would it be beneficial branding if someone kept my Z-Card in their office drawer for several years and, because of its thickness, it would be prominent? That, in my opinion, would be OUTSTANDING BRANDING!

If you decide to proceed ahead and get a Z-Card produced for you, here's the way I suggest you give it to people. When they ask for your business card, hand over your Z-Card. Unless they've seen one before, which is highly unlikely, they will ask why it's so thick. Here's the response I suggest, "It's just my business card. Please put that away for now. You can look at it later. Let's talk about you." They'll put it in their pocket or purse and guess what they'll do when they leave the room. They'll spend about 15 minutes looking at your Z-Card.

My guess is that your competition doesn't even know about the Z-Card. When everyone else is easily forgotten, I want you to be remembered in a very good way for a long time to come. The Z-Card is a great way to do so!

This is another way for you to be different and to **STAND OUT, DOMINATE, and PROSPER!**

Chapter 13:
Hand-Written Note Cards

If you haven't gotten fired up about the branding ideas that I've already shared with you, you should put on an asbestos suit for this one. It's that hot! It's an old idea that has so gone out of style that it's brand new.

I'm talking about the hand-written note card. Most people haven't seen one since it took two sea shells to park your dinosaur. But we're not going to use this branding tool haphazardly. Since I've had a chance to test my branding ideas in front of over 25,000 CEO's in nearly 20 years, I'm going to give you the most powerful and productive way to use note cards.

Do not use note cards with your company logo. You might say, "Wait just a minute Boaz, you slick-lipped foreigner, we just printed 10,000 with our company logo!" My response is this: throw them away. I'll make it worth your while. If you send hand-written note cards, with your company logo, the recipient will think that you have a bunch of those, and you send them to everyone.

Get blank note cards with blank envelopes at a local drug store. The ones which have a design on the front, and are blank inside. By using those, the recipient might think that you went out and personally bought a card just for them. People who are really good at branding do not miss a touchpoint. Starting with blank note cards is another great touchpoint.

Do not write a return address. I want to force people to open your card immediately. If they see a return address, and who the card is from, they might decide to put it aside and look at it later. If there is no return address, their curiosity will make them open it immediately. If you're sending the card to an executive, and want to bypass all secretaries and gate keepers, put the word "Personal" on the lower left-hand corner of the front of the envelope. If I was your secretary, and you got a card like that, I wouldn't dare open it up. It might be an invitation to something important. I would pass it right along to you.

Inside the card, I'm suggesting using their first name, your first name, and simply writing one or two lines. If I suggest you write two paragraphs, no one will do that. I have found that one line, in your handwriting, on a card like this, is more powerful than two paragraphs in an email. The hand-written note card is from you, from your heart. There will be no phone number written inside the card, no sales pitch. This is a personal message from you.

Include your business card behind the card in the envelope. Just in case they can't read your signature clearly, we want to make sure they know who took the time to send them the card. Also, they might want to call you. Thus, your name and phone number are on your business card.

Can you imagine the reaction if you sent a hand-written note card and inserted your Z-Card behind the note card in the envelope? *"Why is this so thick?"* the recipient might ask. And, when they open the card, the Z-Card will fall on the floor. I guarantee that will make an impact. Use commemorative stamps to get even more attention. This branding idea actually has two parts:

1. Friday Afternoon

2. On Your Desk

The Friday afternoon idea came from a very successful businessman who said this idea uplifted the entire culture of his company, and added to his success immeasurably. He has 75 employees. You could do this with any number of employees, even 5 or 6.

Every Friday afternoon at 4:30 they close up shop. No calls. No sales. They put on nice music on the intercom, and bring in a glass of wine for everyone. He told me that no one takes advantage of the wine, but they do like the atmosphere. Everyone is given 2 blank note cards with the commemorative stamps.

Everyone's assignment, before they go home, is to write two notes of appreciation to two people they appreciated that week. One person within the company and one outside the company, a client or a supplier. So, instead of looking for things to complain about each week, his employees began to look for the good that was happening around them.

The CEO related that, within a month of starting the Friday Afternoon program, the culture of the company improved dramatically as they all got "An Attitude of Gratitude". The CEO also showed me a picture of a wall in his office, about 20 feet long, that was full of hundreds of "Thank You" notes for the Friday afternoon notes.

The second part of the card program is On Your Desk. I suggest you have a stack of blank note cards there with the commemorative stamps, the home addresses of your employees, and the addresses of your clients – past, present, and future.

The notes to your employees, mailed home, are not sent on anniversaries of birthdays. They're sent "Just because." How about writing to an employee: ***"Dear Mary, I greatly appreciate how you come into our office and smile at everybody each morning."*** I guarantee Mary will show that card to her whole family and keep it for a long time to come. **You made Mary feel important.** How much loyalty has this genuine gesture bought for you? I'd say about a million-dollars-worth.

I think most companies have a goldmine in their previous clients. They liked us at one point. Why not bring some of them back? Write cards to previous clients and suggest getting together for coffee. Send one note card a day, for 30 days, and see what happens. Adopt this motto: **Never forget a customer; never let a customer forget you.** Your note to a previous client could say:

"Dear John, whatever we did to lose your business, I'm sorry. I'd give anything just to have coffee with you and talk."

One CEO in my audience, by sending a notecard as I suggested, got an old client back after one card. Another CEO, who lost a very big client a few years ago, sent one note card, put it into a FedEx envelope, and not only got an old client back, his first order was for ***almost a million dollars!***

What if you took just one minute, at the beginning of each work day, to write one, short, hand-written note card to either an employee or a client? What if you did that for 30 days? I've seen the amazing results from such a habit.

By doing this, you'll definitely stand out because your competition will think that success can't be this simple. It really is! It's an old-fashioned idea of making people feel special and important. By doing this regularly, you will **STAND OUT, DOMINATE, and PROSPER!**

Chapter 14:
Launch Your TV Network

One aspect of social media that is popular today is video. Otherwise, how would you explain the huge popularity of YouTube? So, in order to compete, stand out, and dominate, we need a presence on YouTube.

The nice thing about YouTube is that you can get a channel of your own, or for your company, without spending a penny. They're free. So, get your own channel and let's make it look as if you've launched your own television network.

Start posting 2-minute videos on your YouTube channel, and don't sell anything. Just become an educator in your field. People want to learn something from someone who seems to know a lot about a subject. Then, get a killer core story. That is something unique about your industry that no one else would know.

You can get a killer core story by going to Google and typing in the history of whatever you do. For example, if you're in the insurance industry, you would type in "The history of insurance." If you're a dentist: "The history of dentistry." You might learn something from a long time ago that others would find fascinating.

Then, go to a commercial audio/video company in your area, where the local radio and TV people buy their equipment, and buy the same microphone that the network reporters buy. Mine is a Sennheiser MD-46, the same microphone as the reporters for CBS and NBC News use at the White House. That will coast you about $200.

At the same place, purchase a microphone "flag". That's the cube network reporters put on their microphones to identify their network. That will cost around $30. Get a jar of rubber cement and you'll be ready to glue your logo onto all 4 sides of the cube. Voila! You now will look like a network television reporter. That will be great branding for you and your company.

If you'd like to see how realistic this idea is, please go to my YouTube channel: YouTube.com/BoazPowerTV. Be sure to click on "Videos" at the top. Then, pass up the first 15-20 videos, and look for the 100 videos I shot all over the U.S. using my microphone. Everywhere I shot those videos, people thought I was a reporter for the major networks. I was shooting one of my videos in New York's Times Square. People were walking up and asking if I was with the networks.

Interview clients and post those videos. Shoot videos at various interesting locations with topics that could be of value to your audience. Take a look at the various locations where I shot those 100 videos with my microphone, and you'll soon understand that you could do the same thing. I would find an interesting location, wherever I was speaking, do some research on the significance of the place, and find a life lesson from that.

I used to shoot with an expensive camera. Now my phone is my camera. The sound on the phone is fine. Your microphone, with the cube, will not be plugged into anything. It's just going to be a prop. Let's make you a network television correspondent for yourself or for your company.

And, when you look into the camera and mention your

company name, add the word *"nation"* to it and it will sound as if your videos are going out to thousands of viewers. The proper line, when you close your videos, would be: *"You are part of the XYZ Nation. Have a great day!"* The impression you will make will be very strong.

And, whenever you post new videos onto your channel, send an email to your entire database stating: *"Our latest television report is here."* I don't want you to say "Our latest video is on YouTube." That's what the average person would do.

You are above-average and that's why you will
STAND OUT, DOMINATE, and PROSPER!

Chapter 15:
The Bomb Bomb Affect

As I've mentioned over and over, great branding is a series of specific touch points that give people the feeling that you are different. They don't completely understand why, but they want to do business with you. Competitors don't comprehend how you can keep winning while they're still trying to figure things out.

Another great touch point is Bomb Bomb. Stranger name. Great service. Their website is: BombBomb.com. This is a way to create video emails that make an impact. Face to face meetings are valuable because people are "face to face". Thus, an email that is actually a video message, from you, has an important impact because they'll see your face, your expressions, your friendliness, your sincerity.

Bomb Bomb is an internet service that makes this process easy and economical. There may be others. I find this one to be quite useful. This service costs a few hundred dollars a year, but I believe, when used properly, could be highly beneficial in making you stand out from your competition, and add to the value of your brand.

Once you join their service, you simply log in, type in the email address to which you want to send, and then record a short video message using the camera on your computer or laptop. You view what you've recorded and, if you're not pleased, you can re-record the message. When you're pleased with the recording, you press one button and the email, with your video message, is sent.

They have a reporting system on Bomb Bomb that tells you when and who opened your videos. Thus, you can tell if your video messages got through to the recipient.

So, when does this service help improve your branding?

1. As a follow-up after sending an initial email to a prospective client.

2. As a follow-up to a video meeting to highlight the benefits of a proposal.

3. As a "thank you" for a new piece of business.

4. To just say "Hi" to an existing client - ask if there is anything more you can do.

5. To introduce a new product of service.

6. Any other situation where seeing you could be of value.

Purchase an erasable whiteboard, about 8 ½" x 11". When you send a video email to anyone, write their name on the board and hold it up for the first 5-6 seconds. Like this: **Hi, John!** When the recipient gets the video, they'll see their name in the preview. My open rates on these is very high!

Be sure to show vitality and enthusiasm when you shoot these short videos. Try to interject a point of value to the viewer. If it's to a client, and they produce a product, have that product handy. You could say, *"I'm sending you this video today while I'm enjoying the wonderful Power Bar you make."*

Bomb Bomb is a great way for you to excel, **STAND OUT, DOMINATE, and PROSPER!**

Chapter 16:
The Five Questions

I believe that successful branding is dependent on one's ability to create great relationships. That can't be done in the digital world or in print. With so much communication happening digitally these days, it appears that the only way to create a strong and lasting connection with customers is to reach out to them and engage in face-to-face conversations. Video emails, through a service like Bomb Bomb, is an effort in that direction.

When looking to create great relationships with other people, my mother was the best example I could ever find. Having come to America with no money, and no English, she was able to start and build a successful business within a few years. Her ability to connect with people branded her and her business as being unique and special.

My mother had certain traits that she had in common with the writings of Dale Carnegie in the book *How to Win Friends and Influence People*.

She was **genuinely interested in other people**. Mother said *"everybody's got a story,"* and she was fascinated by those stories. She felt she could learn something valuable from everyone.

She realized that **everybody's favorite topic is them**. It's not you. It's not me. It's them. How do I know that? Look at a high school graduation picture of your class, and who do you look for first? You. *"There I am. Wasn't I handsome?"*

She understood that **people are as interested in me as I am in them**. If I show no interest in anyone, it is no surprise that no one cares about me. My mother was very interested in her customers at her business and they, naturally, were very interested in her and her success.

Mother understood that **people will do things for reasons, not for logic**. Of course it was logical that people should bring her more business. That's *logic*. However, because mother made people feel important, and special, that gave them *reasons* for wanting to help her become more successful.

So, what was my mother doing that connected her so beautifully with her customers? She asked everybody the same Five Questions. These are five simple questions you can ask that can teach you so much about other people and make them feel important. The same applies to fellow-employees, current, and prospective clients. I'm taking for granted that you are genuinely interested in other people. Start with a phrase that puts most people at ease:

I'm just curious….

Question # 1 - *Where are you from originally?*

Question # 2 - *(If they're not from here)*
       What brought you here?
       (If they're from here)
       Have you lived here all your life?

Question # 3 - *Do you have a family?*

Question # 4 - *What do you do?*

Question # 5 - *What did you want to be when you were growing up?*

Most people like talking about their roots and their history. Once you get someone started with easy questions, they'll usually find it easy to keep talking. Make note of the answers to the above questions in a notebook. That way you can refer to some of the information in a future conversation with that person.

Many people have related to me that they were amazed with how much they did not know about their fellow-employees or their clients. The Five Questions gave them an easy, and non-threatening way to change that, and to make people feel important.

This is also a great way for a shy person to become a great conversationalist. The Five Questions is a track to run on. It's a way to get other people to do most of the talking. And, after all, we're letting them talk about their favorite topic – THEM.

Some companies, when they bring me in to speak for all of their employees, have cards produced with The Five Questions on one side and their logo on the other. They then laminate those cards and give them to everyone. We then ask all of the employees to simply scotch tape the card to their phones. That's it.

Soon, people who were not used to really talking with people, start talking. People who spend time on the phone regularly, with customers, are suddenly expanding their conversations: *"John, I must apologize. I've been talking with you on the phone for over a year. I'm just curious, where are you from originally?"* They get the other person to talk, make them feel important, and the results are predictable: *"Harry, tell me more about the new product you just started carrying?"*

One company, in Houston, doubled its sales in 2 months following my seminar. People were using The Five Questions, which were taped to their phones, to really connect with people.

The Five Questions, for my mother, did not comprise a police interrogation. Her main intent, as promoted in the Carnegie book, was to get the other person to do most of the talking. God gave us two ears and one mouth. Let's look at the proportions.

Thus, since this was not an interrogation, what if someone's answer to one of the questions was NO. Mother didn't want to make anyone feel uncomfortable. She had follow-up questions. If she asked someone, *"Do you have a family?"* and their answer was *"No"*, her follow-up question would be: *"Do you have any pets?"* If the answer was again *"No"*, she'd ask *"Would you like some?"*

The whole purpose was to get the other person to talk. Dale Carnegie said, **"Let the other person do a great deal of the talking."**

If my mother asked someone, *"What did you want to be when you were growing up?"* and their answer was *"I don't remember"*, her follow-up question would be *"What did your parents do?"*

Once again, I'm taking for granted that you're genuinely interested in other people. Otherwise, you shouldn't use The Five Questions. However, when you are genuinely interested in other people, The Five Questions are an amazing way to connect with people, create great relationships, and get them to help you achieve your goals.

When you make people feel important, by asking them these Five Questions, you will definitely excel, **STAND OUT, DOMINATE, and PROSPER!**

Chapter 17:
The Rules of Answers

Branding is a matter of connecting with your customers. Being able to relate to them at an above-average level. Getting them to like you so they want to continue being your customers for a long time to come. Motivating them to tell others about you.

Many sales situations are done face to face. Being able to read people, to know exactly what they said, can be valuable. Many times people make assumptions. *I thought she said this. I thought he said that.*

What if you could become an expert at reading people and you'd know exactly what they said rather than what you thought they said? What if I could share with you a concept that I developed by which you could tell, with almost 100% accuracy, exactly what people are saying rather than what you thought they said? That's exactly what you'll be able to do once you learn The Rules of Answers.

In speaking in front of thousands of audiences worldwide in the past 30 years, and asking a lot of people my mother's Five Questions, I realized early on that I was making some big mistakes with the answers people gave me. And, in many cases, I misjudged.

I would jump to conclusions. I would take things for granted. I fell in love with potential. And, in many cases, I found out I was wrong. Thus, I started observing closely the body motions, the pace, the tone, the eyes, and other aspects of people's answers. I noticed certain patterns that were repeated over and over.

From those patterns, I formed a concept that I call The Rules of Answers. Abide by these and you'll be amazed with how accurate they are. You'll know exactly what people are saying rather than guessing. You'll be able to ask questions that get right to the point rather than going around in circles. You'll be able to read other people's emotions, and diffuse emotional bombs quickly. Here are The Rules of Answers:

1. **An Instant Answer with Strong Words Equals YES** – If I ask someone named John, *"John, does the product in my hand fit your needs?"* If their answer is *"Absolutely!"* there's no question about the answer. It is "Yes" and it's a done deal. That's an instant answer with strong words.

2. **An Instant Answer with Weak Words Equals NO** – If I ask someone, *"Does this product meet your needs?"* and their answer is *"It looks like it'll work out"*, that's not what I wanted. That's not a definite YES. What should I do? Ask more questions. And watch your tone of voice. Gently. We want the other person to explain, rather than feel attacked by us.

My next question should be: *"John, if this product doesn't totally meet your needs, do any of my other products around the room meet your needs better?"* John might say, *"Boaz, that one product in the corner might work better."* Now we're on the right track. *"John, let's take a closer look at that product."*

What if I made John feel safe and his follow-up answer is *"No, I don't see another product around the room that meets my needs."* This, to me, is a great opportunity. Grab a notepad and say, *"John, could you please describe for me the perfect product or service?"* He may be telling me about a whole new direction that I never thought about.

By the way, when someone gives you valuable information, take notes. And not electronically. If I'm taking notes on my I-Phone, I could be checking emails. There's no way for John to know. However, if I'm writing things down on a pad, there is no question that I'm paying attention.

Dale Carnegie said, *"**the greatest honor we pay anyone is RAPT attention"**.* Total, complete attention. And, how little of that do we have these days? Most people are too busy texting to pay attention to anyone.

Once John has explained, in detail, what the perfect product or service would look like, say the following: *"John, if I could go back to our people here and create this exact new product or service you have described, that would meet your needs, wouldn't it?"* Of course it would. And, guess what, John will become the number one customer for the new product, and he'll promote it for us free everywhere he goes. After all, ***people will fight for their own ideas***.

3. **A Pause Usually Equals NO** – People don't just pause for the heck of it. They pause because they're thinking about something or they're disagreeing with us. Watch for the pauses. My mother had air brakes on her words. She watched you closely and, if you paused, she would gently say, *"John, what were you just thinking?"* John might say, *"I was thinking that I disagree with you."* My mother would respond, ***"Tell me more."*** Those were her magic words. When she used them gently, people would open up magically.

Then she would quickly grab a pad of paper and take notes.

Once again, she made people feel important and she got right to the heart of the matter. She found out exactly what the other person was thinking.

The first 3 Rules of Answers can be heard over the phone. The number 4 rule is when we're in person.

4. Eyes Darting Away Horizontally Usually Equals NO – I'm not talking about someone looking to the upper right or lower right. They going back to their memory. I'm talking about a slight move of the eyes, either right or left. They don't even know they're doing it. It's an automatic reaction of the brain when someone disagrees with us. And, if I don't pay attention, it can take me twice as long, later on, to fix the problem I created when that person disagreed with me, and I didn't notice. The bottom line of the Rules of Answer is: **I WILL SPEED UP BY SLOWING DOWN!**

If I slow down, and notice the horizontal movement of the eyes in response to a question, here is what I should say, *"John, did I just say something to upset you, or do you have a different idea?"* What if John's answer is, *"Yes, I have a different idea"*, my answer should be, *"Tell me more."* Then I get a notepad and take notes. When I slow down and take time now to fix a problem I just noticed in John's eyes, that will speed me up two months from now.

Here's a subset to the Rules of Answers Rule #4. If someone looks away from you at the point of the answer, that usually signifies a NO. With a gentle tone of voice, ask more questions.

The thing to keep in mind, when it comes to you becoming a branding expert, is to slow down. Pay attention to body movements, the pacing, the tone, the eye movements, and anything else that doesn't seem right. When you notice something, stop, and ask more questions.

People have told me that *The Rules of Answers* have improved their communications dramatically! And now they will do the same thing for you. This will make you **STAND OUT, DOMINATE, and PROSPER!**

Chapter 18:

Take Your Show on the Road

A few years ago, in the Winston-Salem, North Carolina area, I spoke for a Vistage group of CEOs at the fascinating headquarters of one of the members. They designed and built tractor trailers that were incredible traveling exhibits for different companies.

They were amazingly skilled at doing this. When these trailers were being pulled behind a truck, they closed up to be about the size of a standard 18-wheeler trailer. However, when they were parked, the push of a few buttons would suddenly lower their sides, extend platforms, and turn into an amazing exhibit for the client company.

I remember seeing one they were building for the Army, to help with recruitment. It actually had a full-size Hummer inside. When the walls opened up, and lifted up, a stage came out. There were interactive exhibits. In fact, a potential recruit could sit in the driver's seat of the Hummer, watch a video screen through the front windshield and, since the vehicle was mounted on a moving platform, a potential recruit could actually feel what it might be like to drive a real Hummer.

These trailers would get amazing paint jobs on the outside which clearly branded the products being promoted. Thus, when they traveled across the country, they became a huge, movable, branding billboard for the company.

If your company has products that you want to get in front of buyers nationwide, and you find that the traditional trade shows don't give you the results you used to get, then why not consider taking your personal trade show to your buyers? Have a PR firm work with your sales team to set up a series of visits to buyer's companies nationwide. People love seeing something different.

I was told by the folks at the North Carolina company that their clients get great attention. When an 18-wheeler arrives at the parking lot of a buyer's company, people get excited to tour the vehicle and try out the products. They even get people at the company who are not buyers to come out, because this is a fun and exciting event.

Taking branding to this extent is not cheap. But neither is sending a group of sales people to trade shows, building a display booth, transporting it to the shows, and then doing that over and over throughout the year. What if this could result in large sales?

Talk about standing out? An 18-wheeler showroom for your products will do that in a big way. You will **STAND OUT, DOMINATE, and PROSPER!**

Chapter 19:
The Mastermind Principle

When it comes to memorable branding, it's beneficial to get input from people who are experienced in either business, marketing, or sales. I'm talking about people beyond your co-workers. People who have no vested interest in your success, but want you to succeed.

Napoleon Hill, in the book "Think and Grow Rich", called it **"The Mastermind Principle"** – good people, coming together, in a spirit of harmony, to help each other.

Hill explained how to multiply our brain power: "Man's brain may be compared to an electric battery. It is a well-known fact that a group of electric batteries will provide more energy than a single battery. The brain functions in a similar fashion."

Thus, I suggest that you look for people in your community who are like-minded, and would be open to forming a mastermind group. Look for people who are successful in business, in marketing, in advertising, or in sales. Tell them that you feel there would be great benefits for each member of the group because you would be using the combined brainpower of all members to help each member.

Set up meetings once a month, where everyone would report the good things that have happened in each of their businesses during the past 30 days. More specifically, have everyone report on what they're doing to make their branding more effective.

If someone is having a marketing problem, have each member give suggestions, from their experience, to solve that problem. Choose people for the group who are willing to both give advice, and to take advice from others.

An alternative to forming your own group might be Vistage International. That is the world's largest organization of CEO's, for whose groups I speak regularly throughout the world. The organization was started in 1957 in Milwaukee, Wisconsin, by a CEO who found he couldn't talk with anyone at his company about problems he was facing.

He found other like-minded CEO's, and they started to meet monthly to help each other. Now Vistage has 21,000 members in 22 countries worldwide. You can learn more about them at Vistage.com.

Whether it's with a group you form, or as part of a Vistage group, I want you to have every advantage when it comes to branding. You'll have smart people around you on a regular basis, who can give you feedback concerning the effectiveness of your branding.

They'll give you opinions on your ideas and may come up with some new ones that could be highly productive. The average person will not take this step to use the Mastermind Principle to help take their business to a new level.

Once you do, this step will definitely help you **STAND OUT, DOMINATE, and PROSPER!**

Chapter 20:
Re-Design Your Logo

The logo of your business is like the front door of a house. It's the face of your company, and is very important in building your brand. An unprofessional logo will give your potential customers the feeling that your company may not be professional.

Well-known companies, such as American Airlines, Burger King, Xerox, and many other major companies, have spent a lot of money to create their memorable logos. They understand their value in their branding. Their logos symbolize their industry.

If you don't currently have a logo that is professional, strong, and memorable, then it's time to re-brand the look of your company name. But, you don't have to spend a fortune to get this done.

I recently learned about an amazing resource on the web. There are probably a number of sites that do this. However, the one I found when I wanted to design the cover for this book turned out to be spectacular! It's called 99Designs.com.

This is a site where graphic designers from around the world compete to create designs for a variety of assignments – from logos to book covers and more. The basic service is $299. You can choose the money-back guarantee program, which means you get your money back if you're not completely satisfied with the designs you get.

Or, you can pick the option I chose. I passed up the money-back guarantee. By assuring the designers that someone would win the $299, that assured that I would get the better designers. It's a contest that runs for 5 days. I thought, "What have I got to lose?"

I had to describe my project, a book cover. I typed in basic copy for the title, author, and so forth. I gave some basic concept ideas and let the designers get to work.

Within hours, I was astounded with the speed and quality of the entries I received. One by one, it became hard to decide which one I liked better than the last one. If I wanted to see a change, or a variation to a certain design, I would type notes to that designer. Within minutes, the changes were made.

Five days into the contest, I had 85 great designs for my book cover! That's right, 85 wonderful, creative, sharp-looking, image-building, great branding designs. I liked the concept that Sam, one of the designers, created when I related that my book was going to be a road map for branding.

I mentioned a highway, a high-end car, and bold lettering. I was thrilled with his final design and you're holding it in your hands. I think my book cover speaks of "Standing Out, Dominating, and Prosperity". Don't you?

My total expense for this cover design was $299. What kind of great logo designs could you get, using 99Designs, or a similar service, that would take your branding to a new level? Once you have a striking new logo, that ought to be used everywhere, especially on your packaging.

An exciting new logo could bring new energy and excitement

to your company and to your employees. They could gain a new level of pride in their company. Perhaps the new logo could be used on uniforms, on caps, on coffee mugs, or on T-shirts at company events.

Every step we take to elevate your branding game, including a sharp new logo, will definitely help you **STAND OUT, DOMINATE, and PROSPER!**

Chapter 21:

Your Company Culture Book

Good branding, as we've been discussing, is a series of touch points: Your logo, your business card, your website, your advertising, your emails, and the way your employees make customers feel, in person and on the phone.

Good or bad, we judge people within seconds when we hear their voice on the phone. An upbeat, positive, fun tone will make customers feel as if your team members like what they do. They will judge that the company must be a good one. Unfortunately, the opposite is also true.

Customers, on the phone, can usually tell, by the tone of your employees, whether they like where they're working, and whether they are proud of the product or service you sell. Getting everyone to have a great tone of voice on the phone is not something that happens automatically.

I think it begins with the establishment of an above-average culture. A great culture is based on respect, kindness, recognition, and appreciation.

I recently spoke for a group of CEO's in Orlando, Florida. One of the member's was a CEO whose company is Kobe Japanese Steakhouse. He was originally from Vietnam. His family came to America many years ago. They worked hard and now have 11 of the Kobe Steakhouses operating successfully in Florida. He told me that his company culture was critical in their branding, and in their success.

He gave me a beautifully-done, full-color little booklet, 3 ¼" x 5", that was their company culture book. From one side, it was in English. From the other side, because many of their employees were Vietnamese, it was in their native language. The title on the cover says: THE KOBY WAY.

This full color brochure's opening page had the following questions: *Where are we going? What do we do every day? Why are we here?* On every page of this culture book there were pictures of their employees smiling.

Other pages read: *How do we achieve success? We follow two important people principles... This is how we operate. This is what we value. Our guests love us because we are...*

There were 4 main questions throughout the brochure:

Wow Service Daily Question 1 – *How did I add fun and flare today?*

Wow Service Daily Question 2 – *Did I engage everyone with a friendly smile today?*

Wow Service Daily Question 3 – *How well did I follow procedures today?*

Wow Service Daily Question 4 – *Who will I help today? Who did I help today?*

Is there any question as to why The Koby Ichiban Japanese Steakhouses of Florida are so successful? They have clearly defined, in a beautiful brochure, with pictures of their employees, what they believe in, and what concepts they promote on a daily basis. There is no question. **They are highly focused on being friendly, smiling, being helpful, adding fun and flare**

to what they do every day.

A company culture book could help you look different. Here we're cooking up another way for you to **STAND OUT, DOMINATE, and PROSPER!**

Chapter 22:
Customers Tell Your Story

Storytelling, specifically by your customers, can become a valuable part of your branding program. It is said that people don't want to know how much we know. They want to know how strongly we feel.

Stories can express emotions and strong feelings. When such stories are positive, and they come from your customers, they can brand your company in very powerful ways.

We can all relate to stories. After all, each of us has a story. Our brains are wired for stories. We process information differently when it's in the form of stories. Stories add the human element that we can relate to and they give us a picture we can think about. I think it should be part of your marketing to make your brand stand out.

In my speaking engagements around the world, people remember the stories I tell rather than any deep psychological thought processes. They make a mental note of the fact that my parents went from Europe to Israel in 1935 as pioneers. That my father grew up in poverty in Austria, and my mother lost four brothers and sisters, and her parents, in the Holocaust. They find it fascinating that I was born in Israel, and came to America with my family when I was 9, unable to speak a word of English.

Audiences relate to the fact that I got fired from some jobs, that I struggled in college, that I've had some victories and losses in business. They like hearing how I came through tough times, and the lessons that I learned.

So, let's harness the power of storytelling by your customers in order to enhance your branding. Everyone wants to see their name in lights. People also like to win something in a contest. So, why not conduct a contest with your customers, and put up some enticing prizes that might involve your products.

In order to enter the contest, customers would have to submit a video of themselves using a product you produce or benefiting from a service you provide. Each person entering the contest would be required to sign a video release, which you would have on your website. They would then upload their video onto your website.

With the video release, which would state that they are not being paid for the video, you'll be able to post the best of these on your YouTube Channel.

These could be great testimonials for your product or service. They would go a long way to solidify your brand, and to give the human connection between your company, your products, and your customers.

Once again, this is another great way for you to
STAND OUT, DOMINATE, and PROSPER!

Chapter 23:
The Signs of Leadership

Great branding that makes a good impression, and results in loyal customers for years to come, is not something that continues without a daily effort to keep it going. Thus, companies that possess great branding, make it a part of their culture.

Whether you have a company with a few employees, or hundreds, there are a few simple steps that you can take to keep great branding on the minds of everyone.

Go to a FedEx Office, and get a banner made, perhaps 8 feet wide for impact. Have the following put on that banner, along with your logo:

We focus on Great Branding Every Day In Everything We Do – We Are the Competition our Competitors Fear!

Place that banner where all of your employees will see it every day. Make this the mental attitude of your company and watch how much more focus there will be on great branding every day.

I suggest that, instead of worrying about our competition, let's take the stance that YOU should be the one your competitors fear! Why not? That will never happen if we don't start declaring it, and start operating daily as if that is exactly what is happening.

Another sign that can help keep that Championship attitude in the minds of your team members is one that originates in the football locker room at Notre Dame. It was in the movie "Rudy". Their sign says, "Play like a Champion Today". In order to make this an ongoing thought, I suggest you make 8 ½ x 11 signs with the following wording along with your logo:

Every Day I Play Like a Champion!

Make these signs with black lettering on bright yellow paper and then laminate them. Yellow and black are the greatest contrasting colors in advertising.

Ask all of your team members to post these signs in their offices, and to touch them every day. The mental impression is instant: "Every day is important. Life is like a game. I play it well, like a Champion!"

Post one on your office door. Touch your sign every time you step into your office. That will be a strong message to your team members that you take this commitment very seriously, and perhaps they should do the same.

Let's keep our attitude about strong branding, and an exceptional attitude, in the forefront of everyone's mind every day. That way, everyone will make an effort to keep moving in these directions on a regular basis.

When people come to visit your company, and comment on the yellow Champion signs all over the place, ask them if they want a few to post at their company. Most people would probably say "Yes!" Give them several copies of your sign. Since you will have had these laminated, with your company logo on them, the recipient will not think to make their own signs. They'll simply post your sign, with your logo on it, in their office! You won't know how powerful this move is until you walk into a client's office and see your sign, with your logo, posted on their walls!

When you do this, it will definitely help you **STAND OUT, DOMINATE, and PROSPER!**

Chapter 24:
Be Reachable

Branding that is memorable can be as simple as making it easy for people to actually reach you. Every step of effective branding is essential for your long-term success. This one, I believe, is vitally important.

How many times have you spent a lot of time on someone's website looking for a phone number? What if I don't want to write an email or text? What if I just want to get a live person in order to ask a question? It sometimes seems that people go out of their way to make it difficult to talk to a human.

Keep in mind that every time someone visits your website, they are experiencing your branding: What you stand for, what service you provide, how accessible you are.

May I suggest that you have a phone number on the opening page of your website where your customers will be able to reach a live person? And don't set up an elaborate phone system where I have to press a series of numbers to reach the right person.

Whatever time people spend trying to find your phone number, or having to go through a telephone jungle just to reach a live person, any effective branding you had before is now being eroded away.

May I suggest that you identify your chief competitors? Make calls to their companies, and see how quickly they answer the phone. How easy is it to reach a live person at each company? What is the tone of voice of the person answering calls? Do they listen? Are they helpful?

Frankly, I think a lot of companies are eroding any good branding they worked to develop by missing the point about being accessible by phone. Our goal in good branding should be to create, meet, and exceed the expectations of our customers. Being accessible, in a timely fashion, is vital.

Pay attention to every touchpoint with your customer and you will indeed be refreshingly different. You will **STAND OUT, DOMINATE, and PROSPER!**

Chapter 25:
Time for Action

Now that I've shared with you the best ideas I've tested with 25,000 CEO's, over a 20-year span, it's time for action. But, there's no need to try all of these ideas at once.

Identify one idea per week. If you run a company, get a copy of this book for your entire leadership team and meet briefly every Monday morning. Everyone's assignment would be to read one chapter in this book, everyone reading the same chapter, and report on what they got out of the chapter at the Monday morning meeting.

Then have everyone identify one action step that they could take that week as a result of the reading. Each person then reports, at the next Monday meeting, on the action they took and the results they got.

There are 24 chapters. That's 24 weeks to improve your branding in a big way. If you don't institute this specific branding program, what are you going to do in the next 6 months that will take your company to the next level?

When someone's branding idea reaps big rewards, make a big deal out of that at the next Monday meeting. People will be much more creative when they are recognized for their efforts. Remember, Dale Carnegie said that **"PEOPLE NEED TO**

FEEL IMPORTANT."

When you begin to get good results, please let me know. Reach me at: <u>Boaz@Boazpower.com</u>. Or, if you call, my direct line is 619-723-3007. That's also a good number to call if you have any questions. Let's get to work and make sure that you are different, unique, and that you now **STAND OUT, DOMINATE, and PROSPER!**

Write Down Your Branding Action Plan

_____

_____

_____

_____

_____

_____

_____

_____

_____

_____

_____

_____

_____

_____

_____

_____

5 Branding Steps You Will Take in the Next 12 Months

1._____

2._____

3._____

4._____

5._____

1 Step You Will Take in the Next 30 Days

_____

_____

_____

_____

1 Branding Step You Will Take Today!

_____

_____

_____

_____

To book Boaz as a speaker, or to discuss his coaching services,

Call 619-723-3007 or write:

Boaz@Boazpower.com

Notes:

_____

_____

_____

_____

_____

_____

_____

_____

_____

_____

Made in the USA
Monee, IL
20 November 2019